GROSS JOBS
Working with
RUBBISH

by Nikki Bruno

raintree
a Capstone company — publishers for children

Raintree is an imprint of Capstone Global Library Limited, a company incorporated in England and Wales having its registered office at 264 Banbury Road, Oxford, OX2 7DY – Registered company number: 6695582

www.raintree.co.uk
myorders@raintree.co.uk

Text © Capstone Global Library Limited 2019
The moral rights of the proprietor have been asserted.

Edited by Hank Musolf
Designed by Bobbie Nuytten
Original illustrations © Capstone Global Library Limited 2019
Picture research by Heather Mauldin
Production by Katy LaVigne
Originated by Capstone Global Library Ltd
Printed and bound in India

ISBN 978 1 4747 7505 2
22 21 20 19 18
10 9 8 7 6 5 4 3 2 1

British Library Cataloguing in Publication Data
A full catalogue record for this book is available from the British Library.

Acknowledgements
We would like to thank the following for permission to reproduce photographs:
Alamy: Paulo Oliveira, 22 (inset); ASSOCIATED PRESS: Ingo Wagner/picture-alliance/dpa, 19, Lake Charles American Press, Brad Puckett, 8-9; Getty Images: Bryan Chan/Los Angeles Times, 10-11, Gordon Chibroski/Portland Press Herald, 26-27, Justin Sullivan, 20-21, KATHERINE HADDON/AFP, 8 (inset), MOHAMMED ABED/AFP, 24-25, TED ALJIBE/AFP, 16-17, Tom Pennington/Stringer, 12-13; iStockphoto: burdem, 22-23, PeopleImages, 6-7, Ralph125, 14 (inset), vm, cover, 1, WALTER ZERLA, 14-15; Shutterstock: David Litman, 18, ducu59us, 4-5, Lorenzo Sala, 20 (inset), MikeDotta, 6 (inset), project1photography, 29. Design Elements: Shutterstock: Alhovik, kasha_malasha, Katsiaryna Chumakova, Yellow Stocking.

Every effort has been made to contact copyright holders of material reproduced in this book. Any omissions will be rectified in subsequent printings if notice is given to the publisher.

All the internet addresses (URLs) given in this book were valid at the time of going to press. However, due to the dynamic nature of the internet, some addresses may have changed, or sites may have changed or ceased to exist since publication. While the author and publisher regret any inconvenience this may cause readers, no responsibility for any such changes can be accepted by either the author or the publisher.

CONTENTS

WORKING WITH WASTE

Most people are lucky when it comes to rubbish. They throw something away and never think about it again. But for every gross mess, there's a gross job. Waste workers take rubbish away. They deal with gross sights and smells every day.

REFUSE COLLECTOR

Refuse collectors load their lorries with rotten food, snotty tissues, dog poo and other rubbish. The sour smell of rubbish follows them until they unload it at the rubbish dump.

GROSS-O-METER

DID YOU KNOW?

In 2016, 22.8 million tonnes of rubbish was collected from households in the UK.

ROADKILL REMOVER

Roadkill removers find and get rid of animals killed by cars and lorries. These workers handle dead deer, squirrels, badgers and more. They also deal with flies and **maggots**. These creatures love to spend time on or near roadkill.

GROSS-O-METER

DID YOU KNOW?

Sometimes workers don't get rid of the bodies immediately. They store the animal bodies in freezers.

roadkill animal that has been killed and partly flattened by a vehicle

maggot larva of certain flies

CRIME SCENE CLEANER

Crime scene cleaners get to work after a violent crime or an accident. They handle human blood and other bodily fluids. Special suits and masks keep cleaners safe from disease and horrible smells.

GROSS-O-METER

DID YOU KNOW?

Some crime scene cleaners are employed to do other jobs. They clean up houses that have too much rubbish in them.

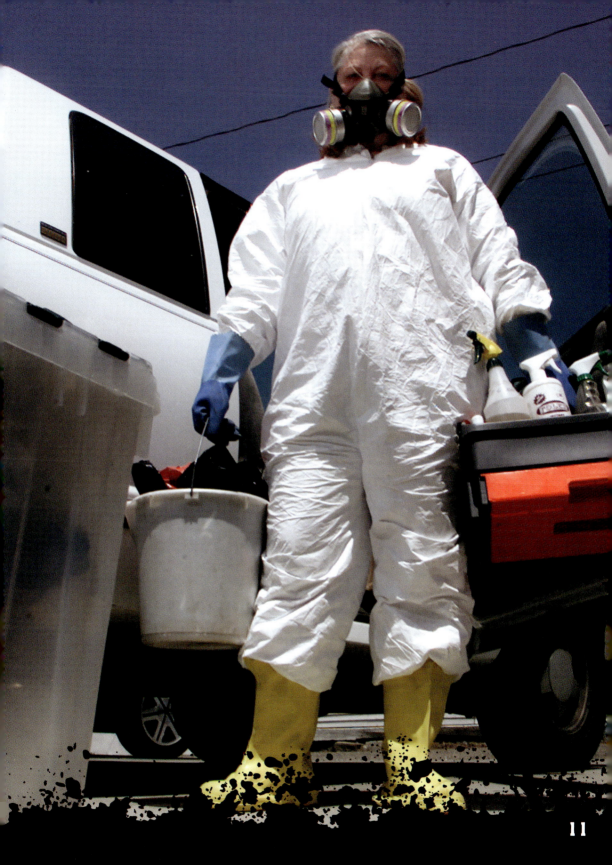

SCHOOL CARETAKER

School caretakers clean up the everyday messes pupils make. Some kids stick chewed gum under desks. Others might feel sick and vomit. School toilets can quickly get dirty and stinky. Thanks to caretakers, these messes don't last long.

GROSS-O-METER

DID YOU KNOW?

School caretakers do a lot more than cleaning. They control heating and cooling systems. They also make sure machines in the school run well.

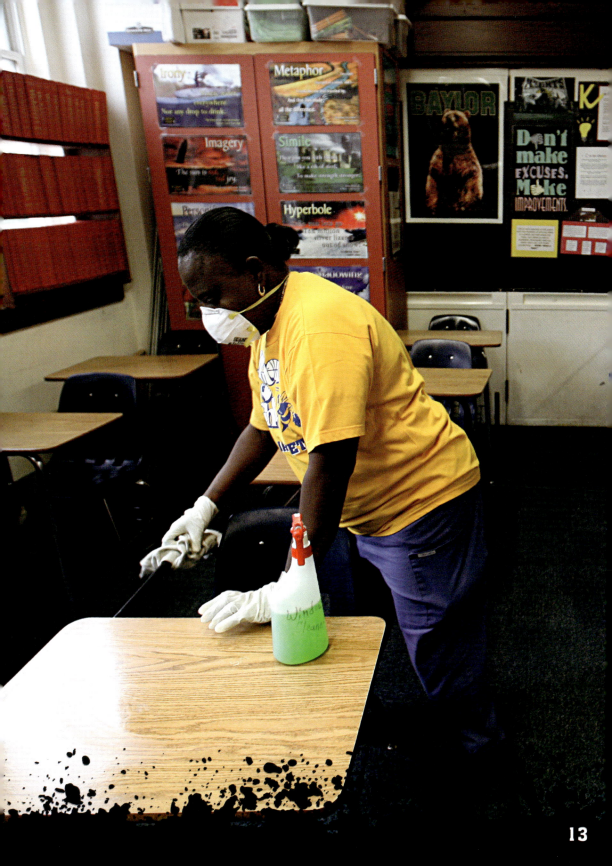

LANDFILL WORKER

A **landfill** is a huge outdoor area filled with rubbish. Tonnes of rubbish ends up there, from dirty nappies to rotten food. Landfill workers spend their days in these gross places. They sort waste and put it in the right places.

GROSS-O-METER

DID YOU KNOW?

57 million tonnes of rubbish, including industrial waste, are being sent to landfill sites each year in the UK.

landfill place where rubbish is buried

METHANE GAS OPERATOR

Rubbish releases stinky gases. Methane can be used to make electricity. This gas is collected in holes drilled in landfills. A gas operator makes sure the gas moves from the holes into pipes. The gas goes to a power plant that turns it into electricity.

GROSS-O-METER

SWAP GAS FOR ENERGY

Methane is a greenhouse gas. It traps heat near Earth and makes the air hotter. The more methane we collect, the better off Earth will be.

methane colourless, flammable gas produced by the decay of plant and animal matter

VOMIT CLEANER

Amusement parks are supposed to be fun. But wild rides make some people sick. Vomit cleaners use **absorbent** powder and special tools. They collect the goo and remove the smell.

DID YOU KNOW?

A company offers a wild plane ride called the Vomit Comet. It makes such fast loops that passengers will feel like they're in space. Many people vomit on it!

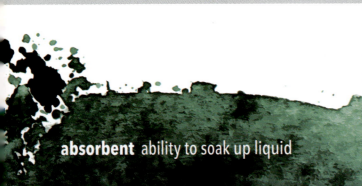

GROSS-O-METER

absorbent ability to soak up liquid

COMPOST CENTRE WORKER

Compost trucks drop off maggot-covered meat, stinky eggshells, used tissues and human hair. Workers stir the rubbish to break it down. In time it can be added to soil.

GROSS-O-METER

DID YOU KNOW?

- Wild animals such as mice, rats or birds may sneak into compost bins and get trapped. Compost workers find their dead bodies there.

compost mixture of rotted leaves, vegetables, manure and other items that are added to soil to make it richer

OCEAN RUBBISH COLLECTOR

Earth's oceans have huge areas of floating rubbish. The biggest patch is about twice the size of Texas, USA. Companies employ workers to do ocean clean-ups. Collectors lower a machine into the ocean that picks up rubbish. Workers sort through the rubbish.

KILLER RUBBISH!

Rubbish kills thousands of ocean animals every year. For example, turtles eat pieces of balloon and stop breathing. Whales may eat too much plastic and die.

GROSS-O-METER

MEDICAL WASTE WORKER

Some of the grossest waste comes from the human body. Medical waste workers work with hospitals. They deal with blood, poo, wee, snot, **pus** and vomit. This waste can spread deadly diseases. Waste workers burn it in **incinerators**.

GROSS-O-METER

DID YOU KNOW?

Workers steam medical waste in a container called an autoclave. The steam must be hotter than 121° degrees Celsius (250° degrees Fahrenheit) to kill germs.

pus yellowish-white fluid found in sores and infections
incinerator furnace for burning rubbish and other waste materials

SLUDGE CLEANER

Sludge is a mixture of oil, grease, dirt and water. It forms inside engines and at sewage plants. Sludge cleaners wear waterproof suits. They vacuum hot, smelly fluid out of collection tanks.

GROSS-O-METER

DID YOU KNOW?

Sludge cleaners sometimes get sludge on their skin. They clean it off with soap and sugar.

THANK YOU TO OUR WORKERS!

Without waste workers, the world would be a much dirtier and more dangerous place. These workers deal with gross germs and gloopy messes to make the world cleaner. Their work keeps everyone healthier and safer.

GLOSSARY

absorbent ability to soak up liquid

compost mixture of rotted leaves, vegetables, manure and other items that are added to soil to make it richer

incinerator furnace for burning rubbish and other waste materials

landfill place where rubbish is buried

maggot larva of certain flies

methane colourless, flammable gas produced by the decay of plant and animal matter

pus yellowish-white fluid found in sores and infections

roadkill animal that has been killed and partly flattened by a vehicle such as a car or lorry

FIND OUT MORE
BOOKS

Microscopic Monsters (Horrible Science), Nick Arnold (Scholastic, 2018)

Reducing Pollution and Waste (The Environment Challenge), Jen Green (Raintree, 2012)

Recycling and Rubbish (See Inside), Alex Frith (Usborne, 2010)

WEBSITES

www.bbc.com/bitesize/articles/zfmm6yc
Learn more about methane.

www.dkfindout.com/uk/science/materials/recycling-materials
Find out about recycling materials and the work of plastic pickers.

INDEX